A LETTER TO ANYWHERE

BY AL HINE
ILLUSTRATED BY JOHN ALCORN

A Letter to Anywhere

Harcourt, Brace & World, Inc., New York

also by Al Hine and John Alcorn

WHERE IN THE WORLD DO YOU LIVE?

MONEY ROUND THE WORLD

When you live Here

and your friend lives There,
and Here and There are miles apart,
or even on opposite sides of the world,

you can still send each other messages
simply by writing on a piece of paper,
putting the paper inside an envelope,
sticking a stamp on the envelope, and
dropping the whole letter into a mailbox.

But writing to friends was not always so easy.

Long, long ago, people
exchanged messages by signals.

Indians used the smoke from a fire to tell
about war or peace or new hunting grounds.

Indians also made special marks along
their trails to tell things to their
friends who followed. A slash on the bark
of a tree could mean: Be careful,
there are grizzly bears near!

In Persia, long ago, the kings built
towers throughout the countryside.
Each tower was close enough to the next one
so that men could shout to each other.

Shouting from tower to tower was
the way people in one place
sent messages to friends in another
place miles and miles away.

In Africa men made up a drum-language.
If an African chief wanted to invite
another chief and his family and his
warriors to dinner, the invitation was
drummed from village to village.

In ancient Peru, people used colored cords,
knotted in a certain way, to tell
their ruler, the Inca, about crops and taxes.

The Greeks trained special runners to race
long distances with word of victory or defeat.
Pheidippides ran one hundred and fifty
miles in two days with a message
from the Athenians to the Spartans.

In many lands men lighted signal fires
on hilltops to signal a royal
wedding or news of war or the birth
of a prince or princess.

The only thing at all like what we
call mail was the special messenger.

Kings had special messengers who carried
letters back and forth to other kings.

A few other very important people
also used special messengers.

A fine lady who lived in the country
and wanted a grand city gentleman
to come to tea would send a note by her
special messenger, who would hurry to
the city and wait to bring back a reply.

Churchmen wrote to churchmen in other countries.
Merchants, bankers, men who bought and sold
things, and men who made goods for sale,
all had to know when their next shipment was
coming and how much of what was in it.

Craftsmen who belonged to guilds, like our
unions, needed to exchange news about better
ways of making things. So churchmen,
merchants, and guilds began to use special
messengers of their own, and before long
private companies of messengers grew up who
would carry letters for anybody,
anybody who would pay.

The princes of Thurn and Taxis,
in Austria and Italy, made a profitable
family business out of mail delivery
in Europe over six hundred years ago.

Messengers like these usually traveled
on horseback and had fresh horses waiting
for them in towns along their way.
Each stopping place for changing horses
was called a post, and this was
the beginning of what we still call
post offices and postal service.

But most people had a very hard time
sending a letter to anywhere.

Kings did not encourage ordinary people
to send letters. These were years of many
wars and much suspicion, and sending
a letter to another country was enough
to make you suspected of being a spy.

Some countries and even some cities did try to operate postal services, but nobody could agree on the best way to do it.

There were many different prices for sending
letters, and there was no way of being
sure your letter would be delivered
on time, or delivered at all.

Usually the person who sent a letter
was *not* the person who paid for it.
The person it was delivered to paid.
And sometimes, when a letter had gone
through many different posts, it cost
so much that nobody wanted to accept it.

Most people trusted to luck and tried to find
someone to carry their letters who happened to be
traveling near where they wanted the letters to go.

Deliveries were still so uncertain at the
time of the Battle of Waterloo, in 1815,
that the first news of the battle was delivered
to London, not by the King's messenger,
not by the Army, not by Thurn and Taxis,

but by a pigeon!

In the huge new nation of the United States,
in the early 1800's, there was something called
a government post office. Benjamin Franklin
had helped organize mail delivery in the
colonies, but the United States mail still had
most of the faults of the English system.
Only a few parts of the new nation
had good mail service. Most parts had poor service,
and some had none, and the farther a letter
had to go, even within the country,
the more it cost to send it.

Mail going out west was carried by private
companies, like Wells Fargo, which ran the famous
Pony Express past stampeding buffaloes and
warring Indians. To send a letter by
Pony Express, you had first to pay regular
government postage and then make another
extra payment to Wells Fargo. The sender paid
the postage, but he still couldn't be sure his
letter would be delivered.

Then, in England, in the 1830's,
a man named Rowland Hill began to
think about the problem of mail
delivery, which was just as
complicated as in the United States.

If it didn't cost too much to mail a
letter, Mr. Hill thought, so many
more people would use the mail that
there would be *more* money for a
good postal service. And a good postal
service could deliver letters *all over
England* for the same price and
collect the price when the letters were
sent, not after they were delivered.

He had one more idea, the most important one of all—gummed postage stamps!

There had been stamps before, pasted onto letters by post office clerks, but nobody had thought of gumming them or of allowing the letter writer to put them on himself.

In 1840, the British government announced its Penny Postage System, based on the ideas of Rowland Hill. For the first time in history, anybody in England could write anybody else in England, buy a postage stamp for only one English penny, and mail the letter.

Within a very short time, other countries were doing the same thing. By 1860, stamps and something like Penny Postage had spread all over the civilized world.

Different countries had different stamps, some square, some oblong, some triangular, and even some roundish ones, in every variety of color and design.

Kings could have their portraits printed on stamps, and portraits of their children and of their great-grandfathers. Countries that didn't have kings could put anything on stamps from presidents to railroad trains to elephants to kookaburra birds.

Postmasters from different countries
got together and made rules so that mail could
travel easily and safely all over the world.

The letter you write today
travels by a dozen different ways.

Your mailman picks it up and carries it to
the post office in his mailbag. From the post office,
it goes by truck to a railroad station.
From the railroad station, it goes by train
to another town or city, where another mailman
delivers it to the right person.

If it is going to a foreign country, it will go
by train to a seaport. And from the seaport,
it goes by ship across the ocean.
And once across the ocean, it travels by
train, by truck, by bicycle, maybe by camel
or by mule, to the address of a
friend in France or Italy or Africa.

It may go by plane, instead, if you put on an
airmail stamp. And a special delivery stamp will
make it go even faster anywhere in the
United States.

What will the mail be like in another hundred
years? We can only guess: Missile mail to Mars?
Submarine mail to people at the South Pole?
Mail copied by machines and sent by radio
to be recopied by machines at distant points?

All these things are possible, but even if
they don't happen tomorrow, think of how easy
it is today to write a letter to anywhere.

If you had a signal fire, and a chain of watch
towers, an African drum and lots of knotted cord,
a king's messenger, and the prince of Thurn
and Taxis, a dozen pigeons, a square stamp, a round
stamp, an airmail stamp, and a special delivery
stamp, whom would you write a letter to?